HOW THINGS HAVE CHANGED

Communication

Jon Richards

Chrysalis Education

Distributed in the United States by
Smart Apple Media
2140 Howard Drive West
North Mankato, Minnesota 56003

Library of Congress Control Number: 20041108654

ISBN 1-59389-200-4

A Cataloging-in-Publication record for this book is
available from the Library of Congress.

Editorial Manager: Joyce Bentley
Editorial Assistant: Camilla Lloyd
Produced by Tall Tree Ltd.
Designer: Ed Simkins
Editor: Kate Simkins
Consultant: Jon Kirkwood
Picture Researcher: Lorna Ainger

Printed in China

Some of the more unfamiliar words used in this book
are explained in the glossary on page 31.

Photo Credits:
The publishers would like to thank the following for
their kind permission to reproduce the photographs:

Lorna Ainger: FC bl, 2, 7t
Alamy: Bananastock 13b, Jeff Greenberg 5b, Pictures
Colour Library 27b, Popperfoto 13t, 28br, TH Foto 6,
28tl, Worldwide Picture Library/Christine Osbourne 9t
Apple: Hunter Freeman FC c, 26, 29br
Corbis: 12, Archivio Iconografico S.A. 4, 30, Bettmann
11t, 14, 20, Mimmo Jodice 8, Chuck Savage 23t,
Mark L. Stephenson 21t
Digital Vision: BC, 5t
Getty Images: Luis Enrique Ascui 25t, Fox Photos 24,
Hulton Archive 11b, 22, Ronald Reagan Library 19t, Time
Life Pictures 15t, Topical Press Agency 17b, 29bl
Courtesy Ford Motor Company: 25b
Courtesy Microsoft.com: FC br, 19b, 27t, 31
Rex Features/Brendan Beirne 10
Courtesy Roberts Radio: FC tr, 1, 21b
Science Photo Library: Sheila Terry FC tl, 18
Tall Tree Ltd.: 7b, 9b, 15b, 16, 17t, 23b, 29tr, 29c

Contents

Word of mouth

People communicate with one another using sight, smell, touch, and sound. Humans have the unique ability of forming sounds into words to talk. Over the years, talking has developed from simple commands to the complicated languages of today.

Language experts are not sure why people started to talk. Many believe that language developed to help early people hunt for food. This would have taken the form of simple commands to organize the hunt.

▼ *Cave paintings are another form of communication, one that shows us how early people lived and, in this case, hunted.*

People can share a huge amount of information by talking to one another.

Words and phrases changed over time as people moved from place to place. As a result, some languages, such as Latin and Ancient Greek, have all but died out and other languages have developed, creating the vast number that we have around the world today.

LOOK CLOSER

There are many ways of communicating without speaking. A facial expression such as a frown or a hand signal like a thumbs up will show how you are feeling. Some people who have hearing difficulties use a language, called sign language, which is based on hand signals.

The written word

Writing is used to record information and to pass it on to other people. It slowly changed from a series of symbols to letters in an alphabet.

Many language experts believe that writing developed as a method of bookkeeping. People wanted to keep track of their possessions, so they started to use symbols to record what they owned and what they traded. These early symbols were pictures of the objects they represented, such as a cow or a sheep.

▼ *This writing uses wedge shapes and is called cuneiform. It originated in the Middle East over 5,000 years ago, making it one of the earliest written languages.*

Writing developed from using pictures to using simplified symbols to represent sounds or parts of words, such as the Ancient Egyptian hieroglyphs. Over time, these symbols were simplified even further to create the letters of the modern alphabets used today.

◀ *The Ancient Egyptians started to use hieroglyphs nearly 5,000 years ago.*

LOOK CLOSER

Shorthand is a form of writing that uses symbols to represent letters, words, and phrases. Because the symbols are simple and quick to write, shorthand is useful for taking notes quickly while someone is talking. Shorthand has been used to take dictation of letters, to record business meetings, and by journalists.

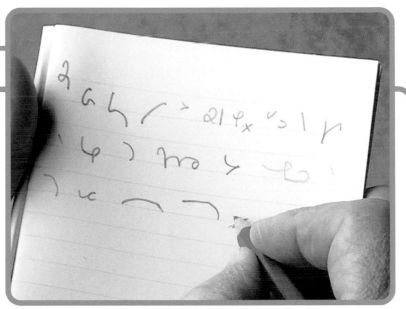

Pen and paper

The creation of portable writing surfaces allowed people to carry around and store large amounts of information. Today, we can write on a wide range of surfaces, including paper and even some computer screens, using modern writing tools.

Some of the earliest forms of writing surfaces were slates or tablets (blocks) of wax. These were marked using pieces of chalk or sticks to record information.

◀ This Roman is using a wax tablet. Writing was scratched into the wax and then rubbed out using a scraper.

Papyrus is an ancient writing surface that is very similar to paper. It was much lighter and more portable than slates and wax tablets. Paper, which is made from wood, was developed in China around AD 105. Because paper and papyrus were light, they could be bound together to create books.

▲ *This Ancient Egyptian scene is drawn on papyrus. Papyrus is made by soaking strips of the stem of the papyrus plant, laying them side by side, and pressing them together.*

EUREKA!

Toward the end of the 19th century, the first pens appeared that did not need to be dipped in ink. In 1884, American inventor L. E. Waterman developed the first practical fountain pen. In 1895, the first ballpoint pens appeared, invented by Hungarian Lazlo Biro.

Sending signals

Fire and smoke used to be the only way of sending warnings and signals quickly over long distances. Waving flags of different colors and patterns were also ways of sending messages.

▼ Some beacon fires were lit in a metal basket that was raised on a pole.

A chain of fires, called beacons, lit on top of hills and towers could send a signal very quickly. This signal could warn of a possible invasion. When people manning a beacon spotted another beacon on fire, they would light theirs and pass the signal on to the next beacon.

EUREKA!

Semaphore is a way of signaling that uses the position of the arms to represent letters. To send a message by semaphore, a person holds a flag in each hand. In 1794, Frenchman Claude Chappe created a system of towers, up to 10 miles (16 km) apart, that used large metal arms to send signals for the French army.

▲ Before the Battle of Trafalgar in 1805, the British commander, Admiral Nelson, raised a sequence of flags on his ship to send the signal: "England Expects Every Man Will Do His Duty."

Today, ships use flags on their own or in sequences to send messages to other ships. For example, a ship showing a yellow flag is telling other ships that there is an infectious disease on board.

Words in print

The development of printing greatly increased the circulation of books. Previously, books had been written out by hand, which was slow and time-consuming and limited the number of copies that could be produced.

Printing originated in China as long ago as the second century AD. In those early days, whole phrases were carved out of a single wooden or marble block and printed using ink. By about AD 1050, small blocks were used with individual letters or words. These were called movable type.

◄ Early books were written out by hand. Sometimes colorful pictures were used to illustrate the text.

EUREKA!

The invention of the printing press is attributed to German craftsman Johannes Gutenberg, in around 1450. Using this early press, he was able to print an edition of the Bible and a number of other works.

With the creation of the printing press in the 15th century, more and more books, newspapers, and pamphlets were made, even though few people could read at the time. Improvements in education throughout the 18th and 19th centuries meant that more people could read and the demand for printed material increased greatly.

▶ Today, there is a huge variety of printed material, including books, magazines, advertisements, journals, and newspapers.

Sending a letter

The ancient empires established the first postal systems in order to send messages and packages across their vast lands. These postal services were the forerunners of the systems used around the world today.

The earliest references to a postal system are from Ancient Egypt in about 2000 BC. The Romans had a postal system called the *cursus publicus*, which used runners and coaches to carry mail.

▼ The Pony Express was a system of horses and riders that carried mail in the US in the 1860s.

There have been many advances in postal services over the years. These include the introduction of stamps, the use of trains, vans, and planes to deliver mail more quickly, and agreements between countries to allow mail to travel internationally. The development of machinery to sort mail has also meant that mail can be dealt with more efficiently.

▲ *Today, machines and computers do a lot of the work in postal depots.*

EUREKA!

The first stamps were issued in Britain in May 1840 and they carried a picture of Queen Victoria. The idea for postage stamps came from British administrator and educator Rowland Hill. He realized that more people would use the postal service if set fees were paid before a letter was sent.

Recorded sound

The ability to record and play back sound is a fairly recent invention, but it has become an important part of our lives. Today, listening to recorded plays and music are some of the most popular forms of entertainment.

Since the end of the 19th century inventions such as the record player have allowed people to listen to music in their own homes. Later devices, such as the cassette tape, were smaller and could be used to record sounds again and again.

▶ A vinyl disk, or record, has a single groove that is read by a needle, or stylus.

By the 1970s, people were using cassette players to listen to music in private on personal stereos, and combining them with telephones in answering machines that allowed them to communicate with others even when they weren't there. Compact disks were introduced in the 1980s, and by the end of the 20th century people had developed ways to store recorded sounds on computers and download them off the Internet.

◄ Today, portable music players can store up to 10,000 tunes.

EUREKA!

In 1877, American Thomas Edison discovered a method of recording and playing back sounds. He used a stylus to make grooves in a strip of paper. When the paper was pulled back under the stylus, the recorded sounds could be heard. This invention was the forerunner of the record player.

Distant voices

The ability to send signals down a wire by telegraph made sending long-distance messages easier and quicker. It also paved the way for the invention of the telephone, a device that allowed people to talk to one another over great distances.

The first telegraph networks were developed in the 1840s and carried simple electrical signals. They were used to send vital information for the early railroad, media, and financial industries.

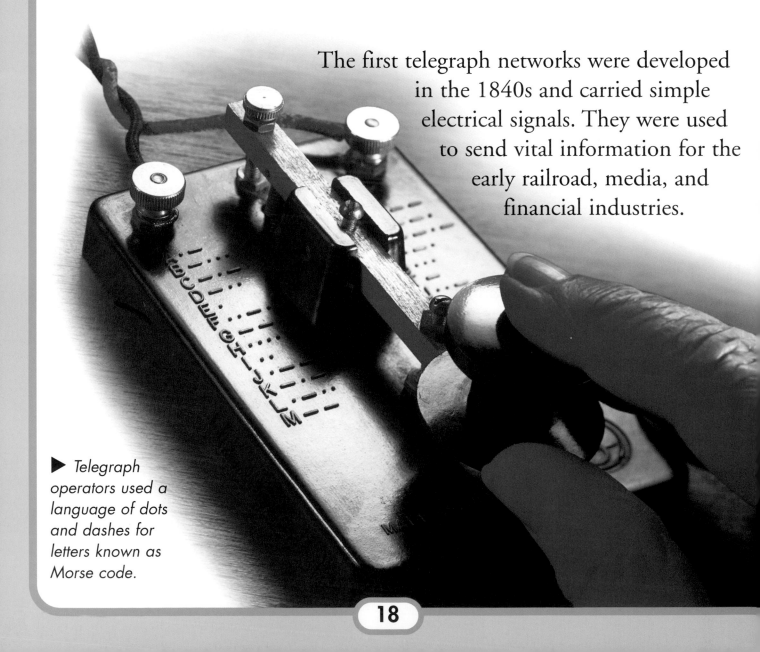

▶ Telegraph operators used a language of dots and dashes for letters known as Morse code.

◀ At first, telephone callers were connected by hand at a telephone exchange. Today, this is done electronically.

With the invention of the telephone, people had a way of talking to each other over a long distance from their own homes or offices. Today, cell phones do not need wires and cables to send signals, allowing people on the move to communicate with others around the world.

EUREKA!

In 1876, Alexander Graham Bell patented the telephone. It converted sounds into electrical signals that could be sent down a wire to another telephone. There the signals were converted back into sounds so that a person could hear what was being said many miles away.

Radio control

In the 1890s, scientists developed a way of sending signals using invisible radio waves. Today, people communicate with each other using two-way radios and listen to radio broadcasts for information or entertainment.

Radio waves can carry signals over great distances without the need for long cables. In 1901, the first radio signal was sent across the Atlantic Ocean; within a few years, radio was being used by the military and the media to send and receive information.

▼ Italian physicist Guglielmo Marconi, shown here in one of his radio transmitting stations, invented radio communication in 1896.

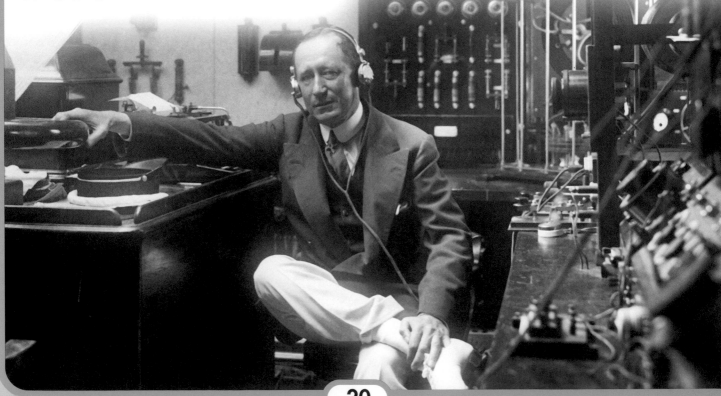

Radios use invisible waves of energy to send a signal. These radio waves are created by a transmitter and sent to a receiver in a radio set. The receiver picks up the waves and converts them back into the original sounds. Two-way radios both transmit and receive signals.

Radios were also used to send news and entertainment straight into people's homes. People could sit in their armchairs and learn about events from around the world without having to wait for the next day's newspaper.

▲ *Modern digital radios can receive thousands of different radio stations from all around the world.*

Moving pictures

People have been entertained by moving pictures in movie theaters for over a century. The arrival of the television, however, meant that they could watch moving pictures without having to leave their homes.

Movies were an immediate hit when they were introduced in the late 19th century. In their early days, they were used as a source of information as well as entertainment, showing news reels of events from around the world in addition to films.

▼ *In 1924, Scotsman John Logie Baird invented a system that converted pictures into radio signals and sent them to a receiver that converted them back into pictures. Using this system, Baird made the very first TV broadcast.*

The first scheduled television service started broadcasting in New York in 1928. Today, televisions can be found in millions of homes around the world. Viewers can even interact with their TVs, accessing information about channels and programs and even going on the Internet to surf the Web.

Over the years there have been several innovations that have improved the movie experience. Sound was introduced to movies in 1926. Early movies were black and white, but some films started to be made in color in the 1930s. Wide-screen movies appeared in the 1950s.

▼ *Hundreds of different television stations can now be received via a satellite dish or through a cable.*

Space signals

The arrival of the space age, with the launch of the first probe in 1957, proved a leap forward in communication technology. With the help of satellites, long-distance phone calls became easier to make and TV signals could cross the globe.

Satellites are useful because they are high above the Earth's surface. From there, they can be used to bounce radio signals from a transmitter to a receiver a great distance away.

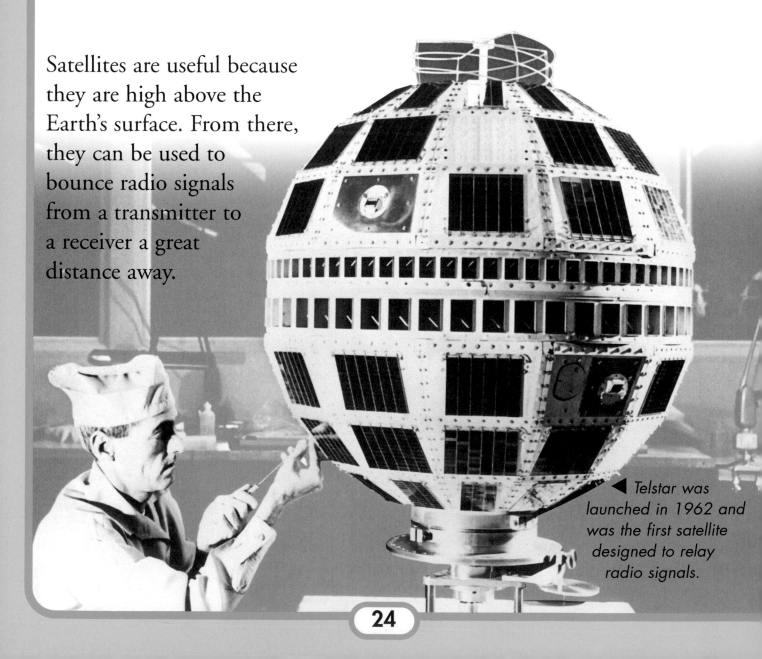

◄ Telstar was launched in 1962 and was the first satellite designed to relay radio signals.

EUREKA!

British author and scientist Arthur C. Clarke was the first person to write about a network of satellites in space that would relay radio and television signals around the world. He published his ideas in 1945 in an essay called "Extra-Terrestrial Relays," but it was another 20 years before his vision became reality.

The first communication satellites could only handle a small number of signals. Since then, there have been great improvements in satellite technology. Today, satellites handle millions of signals, including telephone calls, television pictures, radio signals, emails, and pages of Internet information.

▲ *Some satellites are used by in-car navigation systems to find the best travel route.*

Surfing the Net

The invention of electronic computers in the 20th century led to a vast number of new communications systems, such as the Internet and email. These have revolutionized the way we communicate and share information.

Today, the Internet, or the World Wide Web, contains an enormous amount of information that can be accessed through a computer. Computers can also be used to communicate with other people using email or live video links.

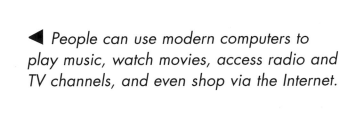

◀ *People can use modern computers to play music, watch movies, access radio and TV channels, and even shop via the Internet.*

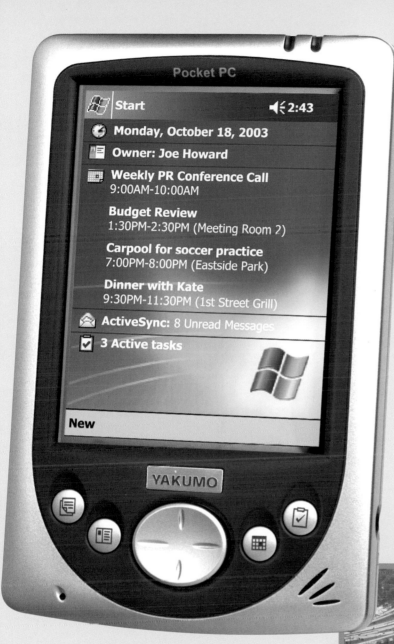

Pocket PC

| Start | ◀€ 2:43 |

🕐 Monday, October 18, 2003

📇 Owner: Joe Howard

📅 **Weekly PR Conference Call**
9:00AM-10:00AM

Budget Review
1:30PM-2:30PM (Meeting Room 2)

Carpool for soccer practice
7:00PM-8:00PM (Eastside Park)

Dinner with Kate
9:30PM-11:30PM (1st Street Grill)

✉ ActiveSync: 8 Unread Messages

☑ 3 Active tasks

New

YAKUMO

The latest personal digital assistants (PDAs) combine the computer and the telephone. This creates a portable device that a person can use to make phone calls and access the Internet, as well as send and receive emails containing text, photos, and movies.

◀ *A PDA can be linked to a computer to download a person's calendar, addresses, and work documents.*

EUREKA!

In the 1970s, the US Defense Department established ARPANET, a network that allowed computers in different departments, such as the Pentagon, to talk to each other. This was expanded in the 1990s to commercial computers and the Internet was born.

Timeline

• 1794. Claude Chappe develops a system of semaphore towers with hinged metal arms to send messages across entire countries.

• 1805. Admiral Nelson uses flags to send the message "England Expects Every Man Will Do His Duty" before the Battle of Trafalgar.

• c.3000 BC. Cuneiform writing originates in the Middle East.

3000 BC

• c.1050. Printers start to use blocks for individual letters rather than words or phrases.

• c.1450. Johannes Gutenberg invents the printing press.

• c.AD 200. Printing is invented in China.

• AD 105 Paper is used for the first time in China.

• c.2000 BC. The Ancient Egyptians start to use the world's first postal service.

• 1840. Postage stamps are used for the first time.

• 1926. The first movies with sound are shown.

• 1945. Arthur C. Clarke imagines a system of artificial satellites bouncing signals around the world.

• 1962. Telstar is launched, becoming the world's first communications satellite.

• c. 1970. ARPANET is launched, a forerunner of the Internet.

• 1876. Alexander Graham Bell patents his design for the world's first telephone.

• 1971. The first email is sent. It reads "QWERTYUIOP."

• 1895. Lazlo Biro develops the ballpoint pen.

TODAY

• 1896. Guglielmo Marconi invents a system of sending messages using radio waves.

• 1924. John Logie Baird succeeds in sending the world's first television pictures.

• 1884. L. E. Waterman develops the world's first fountain pen.

• 1920. The world's first commercial radio station starts broadcasting.

• c. 1990. The Internet is born, providing access to huge amounts of data worldwide.

• 1877. Thomas Edison invents a device to record and play back sound.

Factfile

• The first words spoken on a telephone were "Mr. Watson. Come here. I need you." They were said by Alexander Graham Bell to his assistant, who was in another room.

• The world's very first email was sent in 1971 between two computers at the offices of Bolt, Beraneck, and Newman in Massachusetts. The simple message read "QWERTYUIOP," the top row of letters from an English-language computer keyboard.

• The tiny country of Monaco has more phones per person than any other nation in the world. There are 1,994 phones for every 1,000 people.

• The first computer to be fully automated and run software was built by British inventors Tom Kilburn and Freddie Williams on June 21, 1948.

• The world's largest switchboard is at the Pentagon in Virginia. On June 6, 1994, it handled 1,502,415 calls.

Glossary

Alphabet
A system of symbols used to represent letters that, when put together, form words.

Beacon
A fire that is lit on top of a hill or tower to send a signal.

Broadcast
To send out a radio or television program.

Download
To transfer data from one computer to another, or from the Internet onto a computer.

Email
Short for electronic mail, this is a message sent from one computer to another via the Internet.

Fountain pen
A type of pen, the nib of which is supplied by a constant stream of ink from a cartridge inside the pen's body.

Hieroglyphs
A system of pictures and symbols that are used to represent an action, object, or sound.

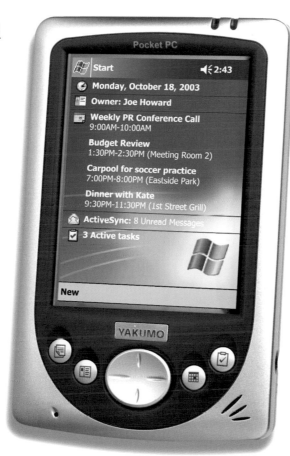

Internet
A worldwide network that allows people to communicate with each other and share information using computers.

Media
The different ways in which information is passed on to large groups of people. Types of media include books, newspapers, radio, and television.

Patent
The official document that states that an inventor is the only person who can make, use, and sell an invention.

Printing press
A machine that presses inked type onto paper to produce a printed document.

Radio waves
Invisible waves that are used to send information, such as a radio broadcast.

Satellite
Satellites are machines that circle the Earth and are used to send communications signals, to forecast the weather, to study the Earth's surface, and to aid the military.

Index